You deserve all the best that this life has to offer!

To my mother, Donna —
Thank you for the gift of life and your
unwavering love. I am forever grateful.
To everyone who has walked alongside me
on this journey — thank you.
Writing this book has been a healing and
transformative experience, and your
presence made it all the more meaningful.

TABLE OF CONTENTS

Symonette Hibbert

I am Symonette Hibbert, a Jamaican-born author, poet, educator, and growth mindset advocate. Writing has always been my safe haven; a place where I find peace, clarity, and healing.

A Piece/Peace of ME is a collection straight from my heart. Each poem captures a moment, a feeling, or a reflection from my journey through growth, resilience, and self-discovery. Fluent in English, Spanish, and Jamaican Creole, I draw inspiration from my culture, my experiences, and my deep belief in the power of words to transform and heal. Through this book, I hope to share not just pieces of my mind, but pieces of my peace and to remind you that true peace begins within.

I pray you find peace!

Symonette Hibbert

INTRODUCTION

I truly believe that the only person who can stop you is you. Life will present challenges, obstacles, and moments of doubt, but at the end of the day, it is your belief in yourself that determines how far you will go.

This collection, A Piece/Peace of ME, is a reflection of my journey toward understanding myself and finding peace in the midst of it all. Peace is not something that simply appears—it is something we must seek, create, and protect. Find peace. Make peace. But more importantly, know that you need peace.

I smile not because everything is going well, but because I know the God I serve will always come through for me. My faith is my anchor, my reminder that even in uncertain times, I am never alone.

Find what gives you peace ; whether it's writing, music, prayer, or quiet moments alone and hold on to it. Your peace is your power.

Through these poems, I invite you into my heart, my mind, and my story. Every font choice, formatting decision, and word was intentional. This book is a gentle reminder that perfection is not required to be powerful. My hope is that somewhere between these lines, you'll find encouragement to claim your peace, protect it fiercely, and walk boldly toward the life you deserve.

Symonette Hibbert

ENOUGH

I AM ENOUGH, JUST AS I AM. I HONOR MY JOURNEY, EMBRACE MY IMPERFECTIONS, AND TRUST THAT WHO I AM IS WORTHY OF LOVE, JOY, AND SUCCESS.

I am ENOUGH

I am ENOUGH.
I am in no competition with anyone else.
Every day I will try to become a better version of myself.
I am special, I am unique.
I have a voice and so I will speak.

I am the greatest and I will always strive to do my best.
I AM THE GREATEST. I AM THE GREATEST
In the face of challenges, I rise above the fray,
With courage and resilience, I find my way.

Through love and kindness, I make my mark,
Illuminating the world, igniting the spark.
I am a beacon of hope, shining bright and true,
In every moment, I am renewed.

I am enough, a masterpiece in progress,
With each step forward, I find my success.
I am the architect of my own story,
Building my future with grace and glory.

I embrace my journey, with all its highs and lows.
I am going to tell you I am in enough in all the languages I know.

In English "I am enough "
In Spanish "*Soy suficiente* "
As we seh in a d Jamaican patois *"mi enuff"*

And so I stand, unwavering and proud,
Declaring my worth, with strength out loud.
I am enough, in every single way,
Today and always, come what may.

I,
Am,
ENOUGH.

Becoming

Each day, I step boldly into my purpose. I am capable, I am growing, and I am committed to living the life I was created for.

Monday

The day I knew I had to pivot,
This is not it, this is not the life I want.
I am free-spirited,
I want to travel the world,
Change lives, feel the sun on my skin,
Dance in the wind, where dreams begin.

No more routines that bind me tight,
I am star , I must shine bright
With every step on foreign land,
I'll write my story, bold and grand.

Mountains to climb, oceans to sail,
On each adventure , I'll tell my tale.
From bustling streets to calm shores,
I serve a God that open doors.

With open arms, I'll greet the unknown,
From every experience , my spirit has grown.
To inspire, to heal, to share my light,
Showing others that the future is bright.

In Jamaica wi seh *"Wah no dead no dash it weh!*
So mi get annodda opportunity fi be excited fi tiday!
In Jamaica, we say, "*What's not dead, don't throw it away!*"
So I've got another chance to feel excited for today!

So here's to the path that calls my name,
To a life of adventure, never the same.
With courage as my compass, I'll boldly roam,
In every experience , I'll find my home.

So today and forever
I vow to live!
Not just exist!
But
Live!

Release

I release the need to hold myself back. I am worthy of success, and I choose actions that align with my highest potential.

Undoing

Ooooh I have an idea,
I know how to make this greater
Aaahmm I will do it later
I will wait until it is greater
I want the lines to be straighter
I am not be best communicator
Nor the best demonstrator
Nor facilitator or navigator
How can I make it greater
when I am a procrastinator ?
Is there such a word as a deliberator
Because I am going to deliberate
Overthink, and overthink and then shrink
What if ... what if ...well ...well
Ok I got this...
Or do I got this....?
Never mind it makes no sense I try
Then here comes the sigh (sighs)
It's better I leave it alone
That way there will be no criticism
That's my defense mechanism
That way I can be safe
I can be in my comfort zone
I can be left alone....
I can be left alone!
Should I try?
Should...I...try?
As time goes by...
I have ideas and ideas and projects
Then I share my ideas and someone projects
Then I am left with projects and projects
Some started, some in my mind , some waiting to be
executed but before they can be executed they are
executed !

Greatness

I believe in the limitless potential of every child. They are destined for success, and each step they take brings them closer to their dreams.

Enough is Enough!

Enough is enough!
Stop telling d pickney seh dem nuff
Stop telling dem dem ago tun kruff
Every day you git up an complain seh life tough
But inna some way everybody have it rough
Mi seh enough is enough!
You haffi tek a stand
You haffi mek a plan
A no negotiation
You are 1 of 1
Enough is enough!
Yuh a pass on yuh low low self esteem
When d pickney dem future bright like beam
Come , come mi seh
Join the winning team!
Come mek mi show yuh Wah mi mean!
Yuh have every thing you need inside a yuh
But yuh haffi start today and seh
"Mi can do this ,
Mi got this
Nah flop this
And it tek practice
Nah sorry fi miself
Mi willing fi ask fi help"
But enough is enough!
And di pickney dem nah tun kruff!

Progress

I celebrate every win, big or small. Each moment of progress is proof that growth is happening, and that's worth cheering for!

Cheers!

Here is to being grown!
To exploring the unknown!
To adjusting my crown!
To reaping the seeds sown!

To dancing in the rain,
And embracing the pain,
To rising again,
With courage to gain!

To dreams that ignite,
Like stars in the night,
To shining so bright,
With hope as my light!

To journeys ahead,
With paths yet to tread,
To living instead,
Of fearing what's said!

Here's to the journey,
With passion and drive,
To giving my all,
And feeling alive!

Here is to celebrating ME!
All that I am !
All I am yet to BE!

Alive

I embrace the fullness of life; its lessons, its beauty, and its growth. Each breath is a gift, and I choose to live with purpose, gratitude, and joy.

Riches!

Este es el año de riqueza
No tenemos tiempo para la probreza !
This is the year to be rich
We cannot be poor no more !
I am excited for all the things God has in store
This is the year of more!
It's the year of open doors
..... blessings galore
Mi seh dis d year wi a go get rich
Let's go , we got this!
Rich not only with money
When I say rich it's not only monetary
But wealthy, healthy
Woiii
Rich, rich, rich !

I want to be rich in the love that I share,
In moments of kindness, in showing I care.
Rich in the friendships that weather all storms,
In the joy of connection, in hearts that are warm.

I want to be rich in adventures untold,
In the thrill of the journey, the wonders of old.
Rich in the knowledge that fills up my mind,
In the beauty of nature, in the peace that I find.

I want to be rich in the songs that I sing,
In the art of creating, in the joys that I bring.
Rich in compassion, in helping a friend,
In the laughter that echoes, in love without end.

So here's to the riches that life can bestow,
Beyond mere possessions, a radiant glow..
For true wealth is measured in moments we live,
In the treasures of spirit, in the love that we give.

Being Black

I am proud of my Black identity. My roots are rich, my culture is powerful, and my presence is a reflection of strength, beauty, and resilience.

I am Black

I am Black
And I am proud of that!
I will not take it back
I said I am Black!!
Black , black , black so what!
I may come under attacks
But I will never regret being black!
As a matter of fact I would not want to be
anything but black!

I am Black and Jamaican
What an epic combination!
Mi seh mi black and mi a Jamaican
What an epic combination!
You know who else is black ?
The fastest man on the track!

As a matter of fact
We are often attacked
Not only because we're are black
But because of the greatness attached

It's no mystery, but let me give you a little history:
From the light bulb's glow to the traffic light's flow,
Inventors like Lewis Latimer and Garrett Morgan show,
We've shaped the world with our brilliant minds,
In every corner of life, our legacy binds.

From the first heart surgeon to the voice on the mic,
We've paved the way; we're the spark and the light.

So stand tall with pride, let your voice be clear,
For every invention, we hold dear,
We are the dreamers, the doers, the brave,
Even though we were once considered slaves.

So I say it again, and I'll shout it out loud,
I am Black and I'm immensely proud!
Through trials and triumphs, our story won't fade,
For the brilliance of Blackness will never be swayed!

I want to hear you say it loud!
I am Black and I am proud!

Being Jamaican

I am proud to be Jamaican; rooted in strength, rich in culture, and alive with rhythm. My heritage is a treasure, and I carry it with pride wherever I go.

I am a Jamaican

I am a Jamaican
I am so much more than "yah mon"
I am a Jamaican
My Ancestors are Africans
I am a Jamaican
Mi proud a weh mi come from
Mi proud a mi Islan'
People ask mi what is means to be Jamaican
So let me see if I can help you to understand
Being Jamaican is verb ,
Because there are some things that only Jamaicans
do
Here are a few
Who else will see you doing something crazy and
blatantly ask if you lost a screw
Or show me a job a Jamaican can't do?

It's also noun!
Being Jamaican means excellence all around!
From the rhythm of our music,
To the flavors we create,
We stand tall in our pride,
Defying every fate.
With a heart full of laughter,
And a spirit so free,
We dance through the struggles,
In unity, we see.
From the fields of sugar cane
To the shores of the sea,
Out of many one people
Our cultures are woven beautifully.

Being Jamaican is a vibe,
A warmth in the sun,
A community of dreamers,
Together we run.
We rise with the sunrise,
We shine in the rain,
Through the trials we face,
We embrace every pain.

So when you ask what it means
to be Jamaican, my friend,
It's a legacy of strength,
That will never bend.
It's the laughter, the love,
The resilience we share,
It's a heartbeat of hope,
In the cool island air.

So let me tell you,
It's more than just a phrase,
It's a life filled with spirit,
In so many ways.
We're proud of our history,
And the future we'll mold,
For being Jamaican
Is a treasure to hold.

Resilience

I am resilient. No matter what comes my way, I rise, I adapt, and I grow stronger with every challenge I overcome.

I can't!

I can't!
The only time I use those words are...
I can't give up!
I can't give in!
I can't lose I have to win!
Let that sink in!
It's either I learn or I win!
That is it! let that sink in!

Release

I release all negativity that no longer serves me. I choose peace, positivity, and a mindset that lifts me higher.

Give Up!

Give up!
Yes ! Give up!
I usually tell you not to give up because you only fail
when you stop trying!
Well guess what ?....I was lying.
Sometimes you have to give up...
Yes I said it!
Give up!
I am going to spell it G- I-V- E -U- P
GIVE UP
Before you put me out
Please Hear me out
Give up self doubt ,
Because you always figure it out
Give up procrastination,
With it you can't get to your destination
Give up Self sabotage,
They know why they put you in charge
Give up inferiority complex,
And show up everyday as your best
Give up the people holding you back
And get back on track
Give up negativity
And embrace positivity
Give up worrying,
That takes you no where
Also let go off fear
Because your breakthrough is near
It is your life , you have to steer
Stay aware, decree and declare
That your future is bright my dear!
So give up the things holding you back
Right now ... let's go clickity clacking clack!

Healing

I allow myself to feel, to mourn, and to heal. Grief is a reflection of deep love, and I honor both the pain and the precious memories.

That phone call !

It was August 15, y'all,
When I got the call
That would change it all.
My sis said, "Dad is gone,"
And in that moment,
Everything began to fall.

How am I a chile in winter,
Yet instantly felt hot?
Heat rising in my belly,
Pulsing like a knot.
What did I hear? Did I hear it right?
What? What did she say?
How? How could this be?

He just told me that he loved me,
Just yesterday on the phone.
Gone? How could he be gone?
Gone? How do you mean he's gone?
I said, "Aaaaaasahm no..."
No, no, no, no, no, no, no.

Hmmmmmmm, no,
I am 3,346 miles away,
This must be a prank!
Some cruel, twisted play.
Gone ....
The word echoed,
A chilling refrain,
Like a storm rolling in,
Bringing only pain.

Yet in the shadows of sorrow,
His legacy lives through me,
Every time you see my face,
Know I bring him with me.
His laughter, his spirit,
In my heart, they reside,
A bond that transcends,
A love that won't hide.

Memories flashed like lightning,
Moments we shared,
Laughter, warmth, and stories,
Too precious to be compared.
The world felt heavy,
A weight on my chest,
The call was a thief,
Stealing joy, stealing rest.

But love, oh love,
Is a flame that won't die,
Though he's gone from this world,
In my heart, he'll always fly.
So I'll honor his memory,
In each tear, each sigh,
Through whispers of wind,
In the stars up high.

That phone call may shatter,
But love can't be lost,
In the echo of voices,
I'll carry the cost.
With every step forward,
In the light and the dark,
His essence will guide me,
A flame, a spark.
To my dad ,my first love
I will continue to make you smile from up above!

Joy

I am anchored in peace. No matter the chaos around me, I protect my mind, honor my limits, and return to calm with every breath I take.

WHEN I SHOULD HAVE LOST MY MIND ?

When I should have lost my mind....
When ? Which time?
When you laid on the floor crying?
Or when you saw your grand aunt dying?
When?
When you lost someone who you taught was
your friend?
Or when you realized you will never see your dad
again?
when....?
When your mom got a stroke or the days when
you felt like you couldn't cope?
When?
When you were told that your mom would need a
medic or when your sister was killed and it left
you all in a panic,
Or when you worry so much that you get a panic
attack
That's takes you off track....
Or then again it could be when you procrastinate
or fail to navigate,
The tests after tests after tests , the trials ,
denials , betrayals...
Can you imagine having to show to university the
next day
When the night before you learnt that your dad
passed away?

Or when you are the teacher in school and life is going left but you have to keep your cool
You can't go in class and act a fool
Keeping going that's a part of the rule
WHEN?
When you let down yourself or when you settle for less?
Or the when you didn't show up as your best
Or when you makes steps forward then regress
When , when should you have lost your mind ?
When ? Tell me when!
Then again.........
Don't they say God gives his battles to his strongest soldiers...?
I guess that's why you have to overcome boulders
Not stones, not rocks but big cracks
Attacks after attacks after attacks

I must say I can withstand
A lot
Because I lot I had to see, hear, feel , be
while it felt like the earth shifted under me...
I can't lose my mind and I won't ....
I can't!
I won't!
I can't!
I will overcome even if some days I am numb and I scroll for fun,
I will overcome. I will not lose my mind!
You fail when you stop trying ... so another day I live I appreciate... I will navigate...this ... life ... one day at a time , one step at a time and I will not lose my mind.

Connected

I am aligned with people who uplift, understand, and empower me. My true tribe finds me as I embrace my authentic self

Tribe

Do know that excitement when you do something
you love?
Or when you meet people with whom you
connect?
The joy they bring
The understanding
The vibes , it's an extraordinary thing!
When I do the things that excites my soul
It's beauty, it's a sight to behold
I can't explain the feeling
It like I am touching the ceiling
It's like I can feel all my feelings
It like a different form of healing
A burst of energy,
My life has new meaning .
Especially when I realize I am not dreaming
These are my people!
This is my vibe!
With this person or these persons I thrive
In these moments I get it , I get the drive
I know I will survive
I come alive
Alive ! I feel alive!
It may be on the street
Or at an event like this
But I promise
You will be when you find your tribe
You will come alive
You will come alive.
So who is in your tribe?

Purpose

I am aligned with my purpose. Every step I take brings me closer to who I'm meant to be.

A LIFE SPELLED IN PURPOSE

Striving for change, I embrace every role,
Yearning to uplift, to inspire, to console.
Multilingual spirit, connecting with grace,
Open to learning, I cherish each place.
Nurturing minds, I plant seeds of bright hope,
Empowering others, helping them cope.
Teaching with passion, I light up the way,
Transforming the future, come what may.
Every breakthrough fuels my desire to grow,

Happiness found in the impact I sow.
In every classroom, I spark the flame,
Believing in dreams, I call out each name.
Breaking down barriers, I stand up and fight,
Engaging my community, spreading the light.
Resilient and bold, I rise to each test,
Together, we'll flourish ; my mission, my quest.

Affirmations

Undoing

- I release the need to hold myself back. I am worthy of success, and I choose actions that align with my highest potential.

Becoming

- Each day, I step boldly into my purpose. I am capable, I am growing, and I am committed to living the life I was created for.

Greatness

- I believe in the limitless potential of every child. They are destined for success, and each step they take brings them closer to their dreams.

Progress

- I celebrate every win, big or small. Each moment of progress is proof that growth is happening, and that's worth cheering for!

Being Black

- I am proud of my Black identity. My roots are rich, my culture is powerful, and my presence is a reflection of strength, beauty, and resilience.

Alive

- I embrace the fullness of life; its lessons, its beauty, and its growth. Each breath is a gift, and I choose to live with purpose, gratitude, and joy.

Being Jamaican

- I am proud to be Jamaican; rooted in strength, rich in culture, and alive with rhythm. My heritage is a treasure, and I carry it with pride wherever I go.

Resilience

- I am resilient. No matter what comes my way, I rise, I adapt, and I grow stronger with every challenge I overcome.

Release

- I release all negativity that no longer serves me. I choose peace, positivity, and a mindset that lifts me higher.

Connected

- I am aligned with people who uplift, understand, and empower me. My true tribe finds me as I embrace my authentic self.

I Am Enough

- I am enough, just as I am. I honor my journey, embrace my imperfections, and trust that who I am is worthy of love, joy, and success.

Honor

- I honor the cycle of life and death. In every ending, there is love, memory, and transformation. I find peace in knowing that the spirit lives on.

Healing

- I allow myself to feel, to mourn, and to heal. Grief is a reflection of deep love, and I honor both the pain and the precious memories.

Joy

- I am anchored in peace. No matter the chaos around me, I protect my mind, honor my limits, and return to calm with every breath I take.

Purpose

- I am aligned with my purpose. Every step I take brings me closer to who I'm meant to be.